I'M A FUTURE CHEMIST!

Written By
Manisha Nayak

Illustrated By
Eliz Ong

WS Education

NEW JERSEY • LONDON • SINGAPORE • GENEVA • BEIJING • SHANGHAI • TAIPEI • CHENNAI

Published by
WS Education Pte. Ltd.
5 Toh Tuck Link, Singapore 596224

National Library Board, Singapore Cataloguing in Publication Data
Name(s): Nayak, Manisha. | Ong, Eliz, illustrator.
Title: I'm a future chemist! / written by Manisha Nayak ; illustrated by Eliz Ong.
Other Title(s): I'm a future scientist!
Description: Singapore : WS Education, [2026]
Identifier(s): ISBN 978-981-98-1042-0 (hardcover) | 978-981-98-1043-7 (paperback) | 978-981-98-1044-4 (book for institutions) | 978-981-98-1045-1 (book for individuals)
Subject(s): LCSH: Chemistry--Juvenile literature. | Chemists--Juvenile literature. | Chemistry--Vocational guidance--Juvenile literature.
Classification: DDC 540--dc23

British Library Cataloguing-in-Publication Data
A catalogue record for this book is available from the British Library.

Desk Editor: Daniele Lee

Printed in Singapore

CONTENTS

Say 'Hello' to Tessie!	4
Common Chemistry	6
Detective Work	9
A Soapy Solution	10
Chemical Weapons	13
Kitchen Chemistry	17
Incredible Indicator	21
Rain Rage	26
Rust Ruckus	31
Lively Lakes	41
Did You Know?	44
I'm Inspired	48
True or False?	50
Project Work	51
Answers	55

Say 'Hello' to Tessie!

If you thought chemicals are found only in laboratories and used only by scientists, we have some news for you. You can find plenty of chemicals and chemistry in your very homes!

What are things around us made of? What are their properties and why do they undergo changes? Chemistry is the study of all these and more! Chemists study the chemical properties of substances to develop new materials and products that improve our lives.

Read on and get to know all about the exciting world of chemistry!

All the best! Tessie

Common Chemistry

Most of us think of chemicals as artificially manufactured substances that are harmful to us. Scientifically speaking, that's not true. A chemical is any substance that has a constant chemical composition. For example, water is a chemical as it is always made up of the same things — two atoms of hydrogen and one atom of oxygen.

Chemicals are the basic building blocks of everything. Even your body is made of chemicals! The food you eat, such as rice, meat and vegetables, is made of chemicals. In addition, other chemicals are commonly used to make food look and taste better, and last longer. These include seasonings such as salt, food colouring, flavouring and preservatives.

Chemicals are also commonly found in paints, ink, batteries, medicines and pesticides. Think of all the products you use to clean things. Chemicals make up products such as soap, shampoo, dishwashing liquid, laundry detergent and more!

Detective Work

Here are the chemical names of some common substances found around the house. Can you draw lines to match them?

Substance	Chemical name
Salt	Sodium bicarbonate
Baking soda	Sucrose
Chalk	Dihydrogen oxide
Water	Acetylsalicylic acid
Sugar	Sodium chloride
Aspirin	Calcium carbonate

Find the answers on page 55!

A Soapy Solution

Imagine that your hands are covered in oil and grime. Would you be able to wash it all off using only water? No, you'll need the dirt-busting power of... soap! Ever wondered how soap is able to remove dirt and clean our hands so well? Let's find out!

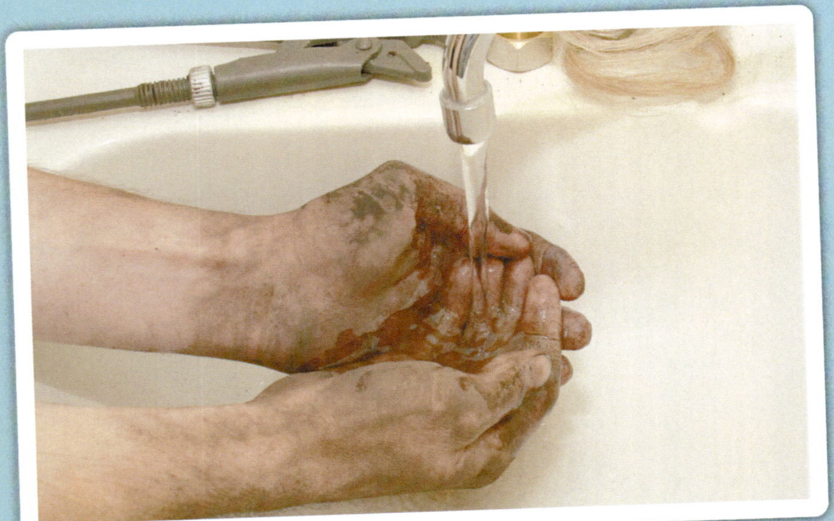

The superpower of soap lies in the special properties of its molecules. A molecule of soap has two ends — a hydrophobic end and a hydrophilic end. The hydrophobic end repels water and is attracted to oil and grease. The hydrophilic end is attracted to water.

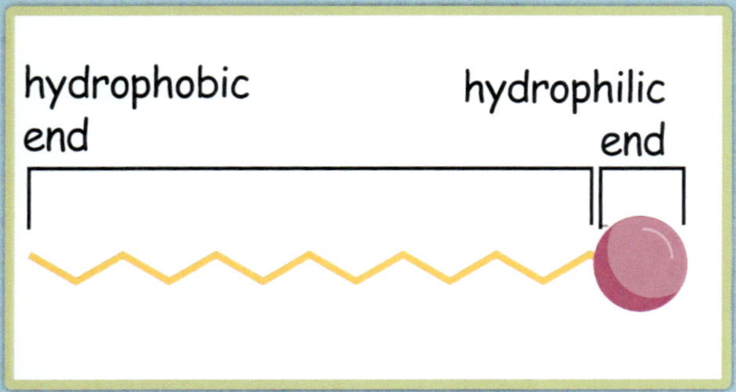

Structure of a soap molecule

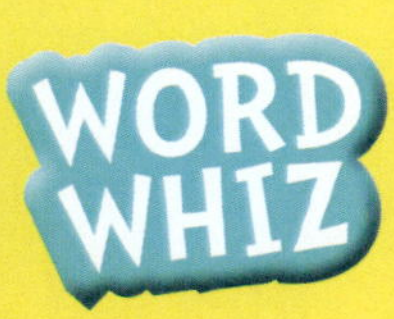

molecule: the smallest particle of a substance that has all the physical and chemical properties of that substance

When we soap our hands, the soap molecules arrange themselves into clusters called micelles. The hydrophilic ends of the soap molecules stick to the water and point outwards. The hydrophobic ends stick to the dirt and point inwards. Thus, micelles help to trap dirt and wash it away when we rinse our hands. Now that's a clean break!

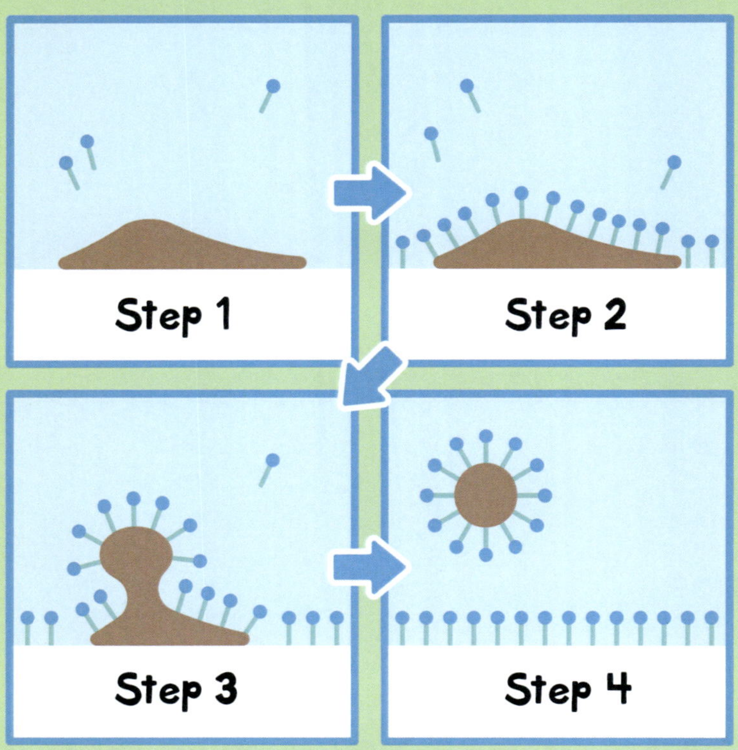

Chemical Weapons

Animals have different ways to protect themselves from their enemies. Did you know that some of them can release special chemicals to do so? Let's take a closer look at these chemical weapons.

Squid

When a squid is attacked, it can release a cloud of dark ink made of a mixture of chemicals. This confuses the predator, while the squid darts off to safety!

Skunk

The skunk is a mammal notorious for its extremely unpleasant spray. When it feels threatened, it sprays a horrid-smelling liquid from its anal glands, which can repel any potential enemy. The smell is so strong that it can be detected 5 kilometres away!

Spitting cobra

Cobras are infamous for injecting their prey with venom. Did you know that some cobras can also spit venom from as far away as 3 metres? If they feel threatened, they shoot venom directly from their fangs. The toxins found in this venom can inflict great damage on the victim.

WORD WHIZ

toxins: poisonous substances

Horned lizard

The horned lizard has a rather unusual defence mechanism. It can shoot toxin-laden blood from its eyes! The precisely aimed jet of blood can travel a distance of more than 1 metre, scaring away even large predators such as wolves.

Do you know of any other animals that use chemicals to protect themselves?

Learn more about the horned lizard!

Kitchen Chemistry

Have you ever wondered why a cut apple turns brown after some time? Or how milk changes into yoghurt?

These are examples of chemical reactions that some types of food undergo. Let's take a closer look at them!

Cut apples turning brown

When an apple is cut, its cells come in contact with air. Substances in the cells react with the oxygen found in air to produce a brown pigment called melanin. This process, known as oxidation, turns cut apples brown.

WORD WHIZ

pigment: a natural substance that gives something a particular colour

Milk changing to yoghurt

Did you know that yoghurt is made by adding certain bacteria to milk? These useful bacteria convert the milk sugar called lactose into a substance called lactic acid. The lactic acid makes the proteins found in milk clump together, forming thick and sour yoghurt. This process is known as fermentation.

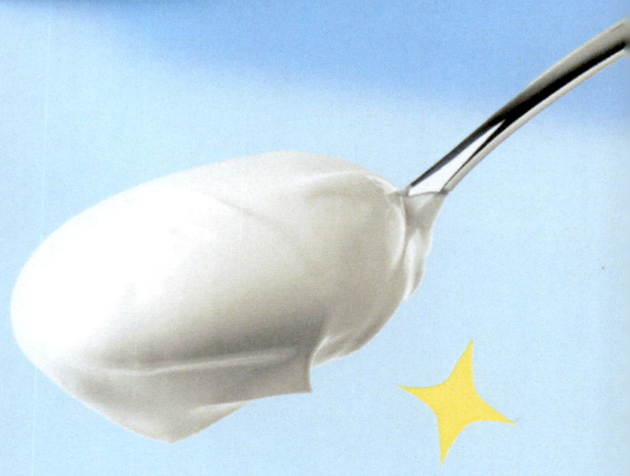

Runny egg to cooked egg

If you've ever cracked open an egg, you'd have noticed that the egg white is transparent and runny. However, when cooked, it changes to a white solid. Why does that happen?

Well, the heat from cooking causes the proteins found in egg to change in structure. This process changes the colour and consistency of the egg.

Incredible Indicator

Some substances change in colour when they mix with other substances. This is due to a chemical reaction between them. These substances are also known as indicators. Let's make an indicator at home!

What you need

- One purple cabbage
- A blender
- Three clear glasses
- Laundry detergent
- Water
- A strainer
- Lemon juice
- An adult to supervise

What you need to do

1. Get an adult to help you blend two cups of water and 4-5 big cabbage leaves in the blender. You will get a purple-coloured liquid.

2. Strain the liquid to remove the cabbage pieces.

3. Pour an equal amount of the liquid into the three glasses.

4. Add some lemon juice to the first glass. Observe how the colour of the cabbage juice changes.

5. Add some laundry detergent to the third glass. Observe how the colour of the cabbage juice changes.

How it works

Acids and bases are two types of chemicals that have different properties. Acids have a sour taste, while bases taste bitter and feel soapy.

Strong acids and bases are dangerous and can cause severe damage to our bodies. However, mild acids and bases are commonly found in our homes.

Acids are found in food items such as lemons, oranges, tea, vinegar and fizzy drinks.

Bases are found in baking soda, laundry detergent and toothpaste.

Acids and bases react with each other readily. They also react differently with different substances.

Purple cabbage contains a pigment called anthocyanin that changes colour when it is mixed with an acid or a base. It turns red when it mixes with an acid, and green when it mixes with a base.

Rain Rage

Have you heard of acid rain? Acid rain refers to rain that contains high levels of acids such as nitric and sulfuric acids. How do these acids mix with rainwater and how does acid rain affect the environment? Let's find out!

When fossil fuels such as coal and oil are burnt in power plants, factories and vehicles, gases such as sulfur dioxide and oxides of nitrogen are released into the atmosphere. These gases spread by wind and react with water and oxygen to form sulfuric and nitric acid. These acids mix with rain and fall on Earth in the form of acid rain.

Factories and vehicles emit gases that can lead to acid rain.

Acid rain can be very harmful for the environment. When it falls into water bodies, the water becomes acidic. This has harmful effects on aquatic animals and plants.

Acid rain can cause aquatic animals to die.

WORD WHIZ

aquatic: living or growing in water, or related to water

Acid rain can be very damaging for forests. It removes essential nutrients from soil, affecting the growth of trees.

Acid rain can take on the form of fog. Acidic fog damages the foliage of trees. It can also enter our eyes and lungs, and harm us.

WORD WHIZ

foliage: the leafy parts of a tree or a plant

Acid rain corrodes buildings, statues and vehicles.

Acid rain can cause erosion of building walls, making them weaker.

What actions can you carry out in your daily life to reduce acid rain?

Learn more about acid rain!

Rust Ruckus

What wonderful weather for a bicycle ride!
You bet, Oscar!
Uh oh, Olive! I think I spoke too soon!

Oh no...
We're almost home...
RUN!

The next morning...
Oh no...
Oscar! Wake up!
Huh... What is it??

We forgot to bring our bicycles inside!!
Oh no, they've been out in the rain all night!

Oh nooo... RUST!
Mine is also rusted in several places...
What's up, kids?
Mum, we left our bikes out in the rain and now they've rusted!

All right, so now we have a Sunday project.
Project rust removal!
What exactly *is* rust?
Rust is a reddish-brown substance formed when iron and oxygen react in the presence of moisture.

Bicycles are made of metals such as iron. The iron in the bicycle rusts when exposed to oxygen and moisture.
How do we remove the rust?
We can use this cleaning pad or this old toothbrush to gently scrub the rust away.

What about the chain? It looks quite badly rusted.
We'll need to remove the chain and soak it in vinegar before scrubbing it.
Vinegar? How does vinegar help?
Vinegar contains an acid that reacts with the rust and dissolves it.
VINEGAR

Wow! We've managed to remove all the rust!
Once the chains are fully dry, we'll put a lubricant on them. This will make them move more easily and also form a protective layer against rust.

We're never leaving our bicycles out in the open again!
Good idea. Rust can destroy your bicycle over time. Rusting occurs more quickly on humid days or if the bicycles are wet.
Keep your bicycles clean and dry. And always store them in a dry, sheltered place.
Yes, Mum!
The end

Lively Lakes

Did you know that not all lakes in the world appear blue? Let's look at a few lakes with unique colours and understand the chemistry behind them!

Pretty in pink

Lake Hillier in Australia is famous for its bright pink colour. The colour comes from the pigments produced by certain algae and bacteria that thrive in the extremely salty lake.

WORD WHIZ

algae: plant-like organisms found mainly in water, which can make their own food

Changing colours

The Five Flower Lake in China attracts many tourists due to its bright green and blue hues. More amazingly, the colours of the lake keep changing. The changing colours are due to a combination of factors — minerals and rocks in the water, seasonal changes to the vegetation around the lake, and the presence of plants and algae in the water.

Red alert

Laguna Colorado is a lake in Bolivia that is known for its bright red colour. The colour comes from the red sediments and red algae found in the lake. The red algae also serve as a food source for the flamingos that are frequently spotted in the lake.

Did You Know?

Let's check out some cool chemistry facts!

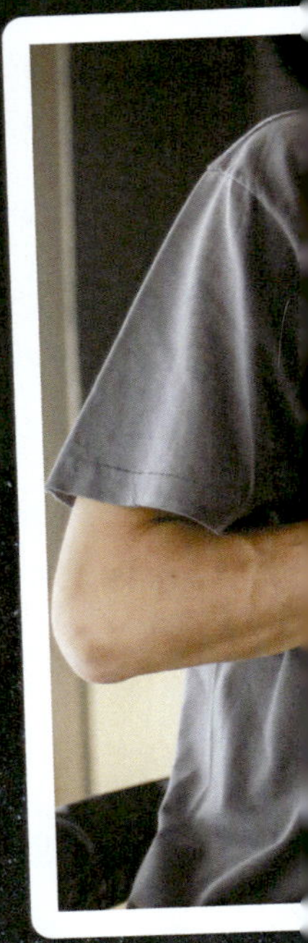

Mercury is the only metal that is a liquid at room temperature.

Cutting onions makes us cry. When we cut onions, they release a gas that irritates our eyes and make them produce tears to wash away the irritant.

Mars is covered in rust! Its surface contains a lot of iron oxide, commonly known as rust. This gives Mars its characteristic reddish colour.

Diamond and graphite are different forms of the same substance — pure carbon. They look so dissimilar because the carbon atoms are arranged differently in them.

The butterfly pea flower contains a blue pigment called anthocyanin, which can be used as a natural food dye.

The famous Statue of Liberty in New York was not always blue-green in colour! When it was first unveiled in 1886, it was a shiny reddish-brown. Within a couple of decades, chemical reactions between the copper in the statue and the oxygen in the air caused the statue to turn blue-green. Scientists believe that other reactions due to air pollution also contributed to the colour change.

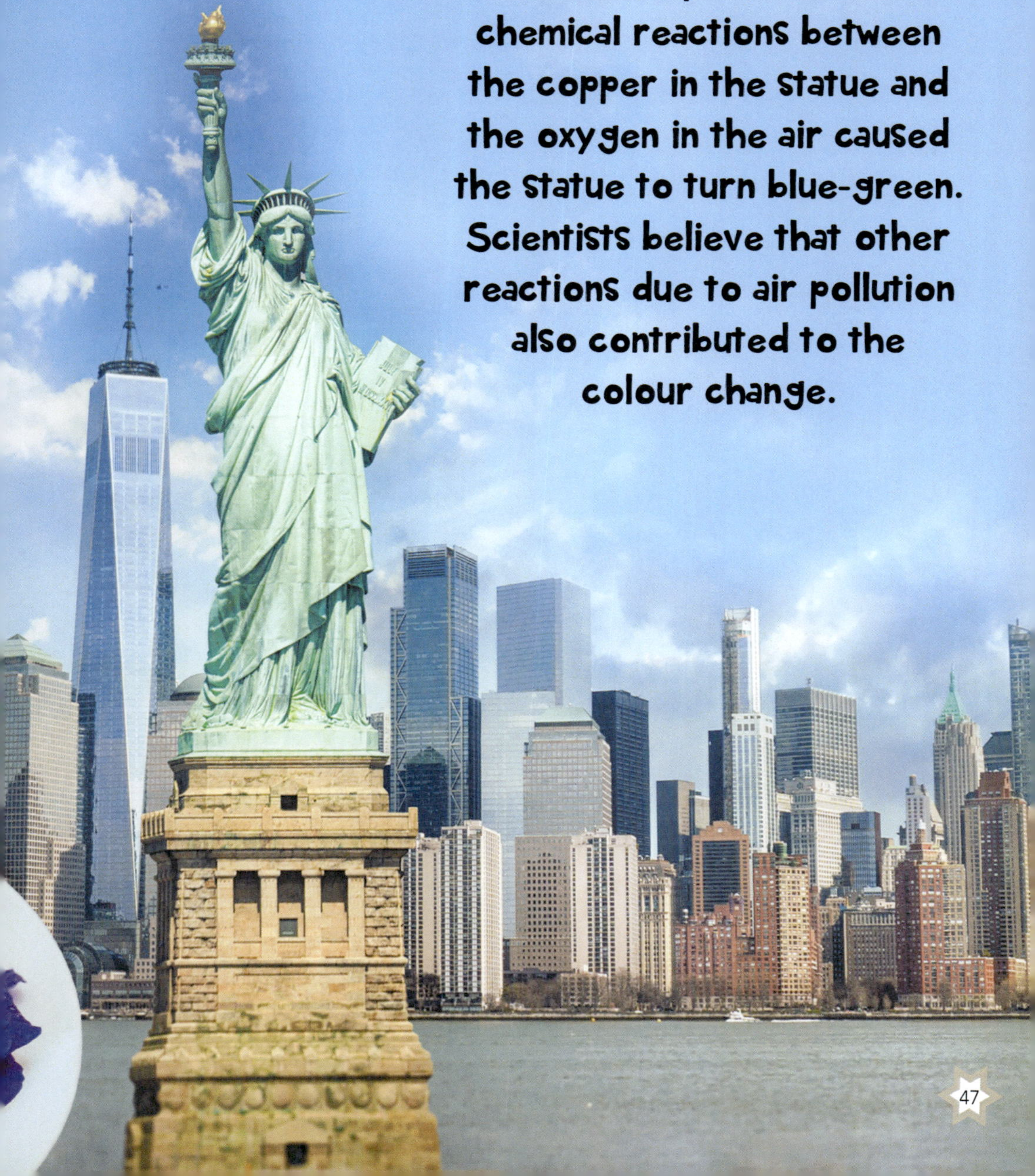

I'm Inspired

The Nobel Prize is widely regarded as the most prestigious award for intellectual achievement. Did you know that Marie Curie was the first woman to win the Nobel Prize, the first person to win the Nobel Prize twice and the only person to have won the Nobel Prize in two different scientific fields? Now that's remarkable indeed!

Born in 1867 in Poland, Marie became one of the most respected scientists in the world. Her discovery of new elements, groundbreaking research on radioactivity and contribution to finding cancer treatments make her an icon.

In 1903, Marie won the Nobel Prize in Physics, together with French physicists Henri Becquerel and Pierre Curie (Marie's husband) for their work on radioactivity.

Pierre and Marie Curie in their laboratory

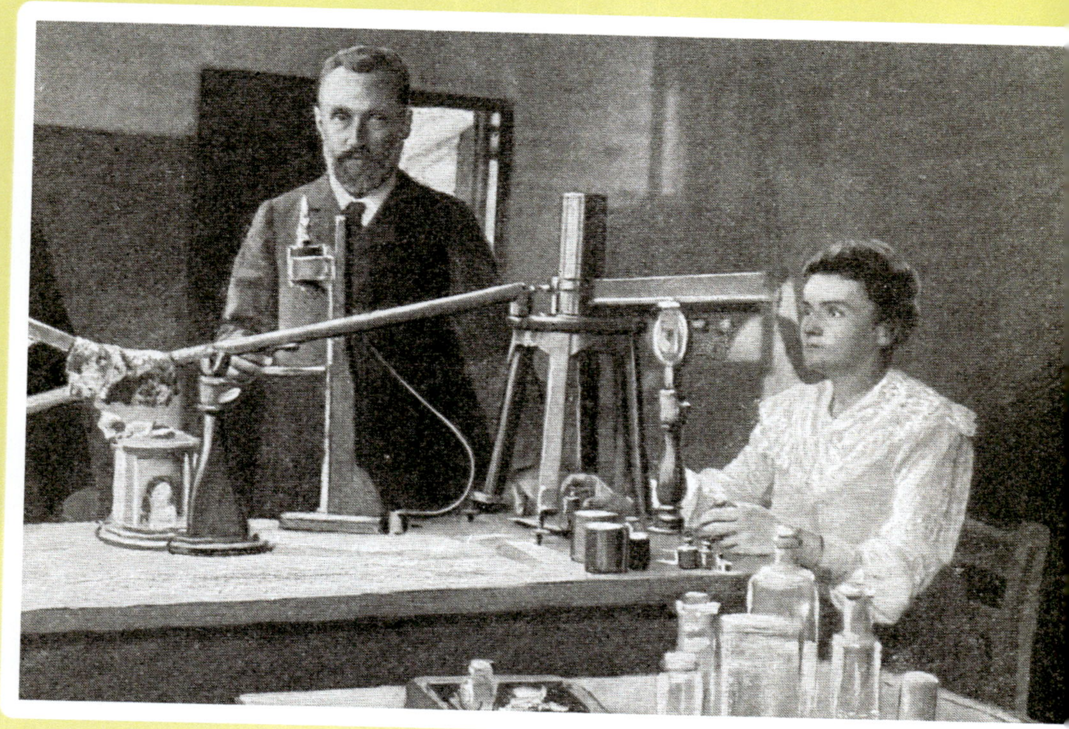

In 1911, Marie won the Nobel Prize in Chemistry for discovering the elements radium and polonium.

Though Marie Curie died in 1934, her invaluable contributions to science and her legacy continue to inspire scientists even today.

True or False?

Do you remember what you have learnt about chemistry so far? Test yourself with this quiz! Which sentences are true and which are false?

1. Water is a chemical.
2. The hydrophobic end of a soap molecule attracts water.
3. When threatened, a skunk sprays a smelly liquid from its mouth.
4. The horned lizard can shoot blood from its eyes.
5. Useful fungi help to convert milk to yoghurt.
6. Fizzy drinks contain acids.
7. Acid rain can affect both plants and animals.
8. Algae are plants.
9. The Statue of Liberty was originally blue-green in colour.
10. Marie Curie has won the Nobel Prize in both Physics and Chemistry.

Project Work

Did you know that you can create your own model of a volcano using things found at home? What's more, it even erupts on command!

What you need

- Safety goggles
- A large baking tray
- Brown modelling clay
- Dish soap
- Vinegar
- Newspapers
- A plastic cup
- Baking soda
- Red food colouring
- An adult to supervise

What you need to do

1. Put on the safety goggles.

2. Lay newspapers on the table and put the baking tray on it.

3. Place the plastic cup on the baking tray and shape the modelling clay around it in the shape of a mountain.

4. Put four tablespoons of baking soda in the plastic cup.

5. Add a few drops of dish soap and a few drops of red food colouring over the baking soda. This will make the 'eruption' more dramatic.

6. From a safe distance, pour half a cup of vinegar into the cup. Your volcano will erupt instantly!

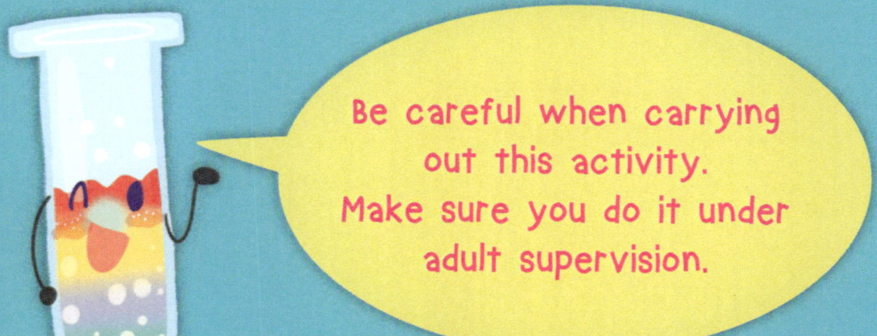

Answers

Detective Work (page 9)

Salt - Sodium chloride

Baking soda - Sodium bicarbonate

Chalk - Calcium carbonate

Water - Dihydrogen oxide

Sugar - Sucrose

Aspirin - Acetylsalicylic acid

True or False? (page 50)

1. True
2. False
3. False
4. True
5. False
6. True
7. True
8. False
9. False
10. True

I'M A FUTURE SCIENTIST!

The I'm a Future Scientist! series of full-colour books for 6–12 year olds will spark sustained interest in scientific fields, such as botany, zoology, marine biology, conservation and the environment, astronomy, and many more, delivering primary-school-level Science learning points in an engaging and relatable way! Through clearly written educational articles, fun cartoons, suggested hands-on activities, as well as full-colour photographs and illustrations, these books are the perfect companions for budding scientists to delve further into a wide range of scientific fields.

WS Education

Email sales@wspc.com for sales enquiries and bulk purchase opportunities.